The Best Ninja Foodi Smart Xl Grill Cookbook

A Complete Compilation Of All The Tips To Master Air Frying, Indoor And Outdoor Grilling With Heavenly Ninja Foodi Smart Xl Grill Recipes For Beginners

Lilla Marcus

Table of Contents

Introduction

N inja Foodi XL Grill Cookbook" introduces you to the Ninja Foodi XL grill and provides you with over 2000 healthy recipes created only for this grill. The book will show you how to prepare a variety of delicious dishes with this versatile grill.

This is the food processor that I have been waiting for since I started cooking. Its large capacity bowl and versatile blade assembly make it an ideal product to use for everyday cooking.

Foodi Smart XL Grill, the latest kitchen appliance by Ninja Foodi, is a food processor that can be used as a griller, slicer, mixer, and blender at homes.

Foodi Smart XL has a large processing bowl of 6.4 quarts capacity that can hold a lot of food for slicing or grilling. The bowl is large enough to make ten servings of coleslaw or salsa, and it is the perfect size for roasting a 3-pound chicken as well.

And the blade assembly can chop, slice shred, mix and blend.

The cookbook starts with an introduction to the Ninja Foodi XL grill. You will learn how to clean the grill, prepare it for use, and then go through the instructions for using this amazing kitchen appliance.

After reading "Ninja Foodi XL Grill Cookbook", you will be ready to make healthy and delicious dishes. You can use this book as a great reference guide for all your grill cooking needs. It can also be a significant learning experience for those who want to get inspired to cook new dishes or gain cooking skills.

When cooking at home, you want a cookbook that delivers. Every cookbook should be tailored to your specific needs, so why not designed for the Ninja Foodi XL Grill? The same team is written by Ninja Foodie XL Grill Cookbook's Ninja Foodie XL Grill Cookbook 1-2-3 series. The Ninja Foodi XL Grill Cookbook offers a practical approach to grilling that will help you get the most from your new grill.

Previous grills have either been too small or not easy to use. I wanted to create the perfect healthy alternative for my family, so I worked on creating a healthier way to cook and grill.

But my mission wasn't only to create a healthy way of cooking but to also make it easy for everyone.

With Ninja Foodi Smart XL Grill everything is easier, and you will be able to enjoy your favorite grilled food with less work and hassle.

While all of our cookbooks provide a great foundation for your grilling adventures, this one is specially designed for this recent addition to the Ninja Foodi XL Grill Cookbook family. We love our Ninja Foodi XL Grill, so we took extra time to make sure we offered the best possible guidance on its proper use.

The Ninja Foodi grill and the other grills differ in several ways. The enormous difference is that the Ninja Foodi Grill heats faster than other grills and cooks much more evenly. This is because the Ninja Foodi Smart XL grill is a solid core-less infrared grill. It uses ceramic infrared burners, which are in a cylinder inside the grill, therefore there are no gaps between the heating elements (unlike most electric grills).

Whether you are a first-time griller or a seasoned pro, The Ninja Foodie XL Grill Cookbook delivers the information you need to ensure that your time spent on the grill will reward and pleasurable.

CHAPTER 1:

Six Methods of Ninja Foodi XL Smart Grill

Now that you have a basic idea of what the Ninja Foodi Smart XL Grill is let's look at the core functions and buttons you should know about. Remember that you have five different cooking types that you can do using your Ninja Foodi Grill.

Grill

At its heart, the Ninja Foodi Smart XL Grill is an indoor grill, so to unlock its full potential, you must understand how the grill function of the appliance works. Let me break it down to you.

Now understand that each set of the Grill is specifically designed for fresh food.

But regardless of which function you choose, the first step for you will always be:

- Place your cooking pot and grill grate in the Ninja Foodi.'
- Let it pre-heat
- Then add your food

The next thing would be to select the Grill function and choose the Grill Temperature. Here you have 4 settings to choose from.

- **Low:** This mode is perfect for bacon and sausages.
- **Medium:** This is perfect for frozen meats or marinated meats.
- **High:** This mode is perfect for steaks, chicken, and burgers.
- **Max:** This is perfect for vegetables, fruits, fresh and frozen seafood, and pizza.

Air Crisp

The Air Crisp mode will help you achieve a very crispy and crunchy golden-brown finish to your food. Using the Air Crisp mode combined with the crisper basket is the perfect combination to cook frozen foods such as french fries, onion rings, and chicken nuggets. Air Crisp is also amazing for Brussels sprouts and other fresh vegetables. Just always shake the crisper basket once or twice to ensure even cooking.

Bake

As mentioned earlier, the Ninja Foodi Smart XL Grill is essentially a mini convection oven. All you need to bake bread, cakes, pies, and other sweet treats is a Cooking Pot and this function. The Pre-heat time for the Bake mode is just 3 minutes.

Roast

The Roast function is used to make everything from slow-roasted pot roast to appetizers to casual sides. Large protein pieces can be put directly in your Ninja Foodi Smart XL Grill and roasted using this function. You can further make this mode more effective by using a Roasting Rack accessory.

Dehydrate

Dehydrators are pretty expensive and take a lot of space in your kitchen. Luckily, you can very easily dehydrate fruits, meats, vegetables, herbs, etc., using just your Ninja Foodi Grill!

The Inspiration Behind This Cookbook

One of my all-time favorite foods is Beef Stew. It's a great meal to batch cook for those busy nights, but it's also what I make for my kids when they're sick. Beef stew is not only hearty and delicious, but it reminds me of my childhood in a way that could bring me to tears. Now, before my Ninja Foodi... Let me tell you how I used to make Beef Stew. First, I would pat dry the beef cubes and season them - this step is a no brainer. Next, I would heat a frying pan on high with some oil and slowly sear the beef, in batches so I didn't overcrowd the pan. It takes a long time and produces a lot of smoke, not to mention, using a lot of oil. Next, I would fill my slow cooker with stock and vegetables. This worked great but took all day to cook and created a lot of dishes to clean.

With the Ninja Foodi, I can sear, simmer, roast, and braise all in one easy-to-clean appliance. The pre-programmed buttons make it so easy, even my kids can make beef stew in it now! This is one of the tabletop appliances on the market that gets hot enough to sear meat properly, so the first thing I made with my Ninja Foodi was beef stew.

What Makes the Ninja Foodi so Great?

Authorization strolls you through how I make beef stew since getting my Ninja Foodi. I open a package of meat, season it, and add it to the Ninja foodi and set it to "sear." In minutes, the temperature has reached 500F so I set a timer after placing the lid on (so there's virtually no smoke at all,) and then come back when the timer has gone off to add the stock and fresh veggies… And voila! In just one hour I have tender, flavorful, juicy, hearty, healthy beef stew!

But it's more than just beef stew! I use my Ninja Foodi for just about everything now, which is why I wanted to create this cookbook (with more than 500 recipes!) to show you how you too can revolutionize the way you cook. You and your family will save time and be healthier in the end - it's really a win-win! (You might also end up feeling like a world-class chef in the end, because everything in this book is so tasty!)

Along with saving money on my energy bill and saving me tons of time around dinner time, this appliance also helped make me and my family healthier! I used to add a lot of oil to the surface of meat before cooking, to prevent it from sticking. I was fed up with losing half a chicken breast on the barbeque so then I started baking them, which didn't offer a lot of flavors. I also used a lot of oil on things like grilled bread, fish, or vegetables. But with the air crisp setting on this machine, you don't need to use any oil whatsoever… which has had an incredible impact on my health. If you're not concerned about oil, this machine will still allow you to enjoy more of the foods that fit into your meal plan – for keto or paleo diets, the Ninja Foodi is a great addition to your kitchen, because of how conveniently you can cook such a variety of proteins.

Making the Most of Your Ninja Foodi

The Ninja Foodi has 6 function buttons which completely replaced my toaster, toaster oven, deep fryer, oven, stovetop, microwave, and even my outdoor barbeque! With this device, I can roast a chicken, a whole fish, or any of my favorite oven meals. I can quickly heat up a piece of pizza or toast. I can air crisp chicken wings or fish sticks for the kids. I can bake a cake or fresh bread. I can dehydrate apple chips or kale chips. I can broil garlic bread or grilled cheese. And probably most impressively… I can grill with no smoke or fire hazards year-round indoors!! Now you try to name an appliance that can do all of that!?!?!

Now you may be wondering – "But is this thing really as good as my barbeque?" The answer is YES and once you try just a few of the recipes from this cook, you will see for yourself. So far, I have grilled everything from shrimp skewers to corn on the cob, to loaded baked potatoes, to hot dogs and yes, even the perfect medium-rare steak. The Ninja Foodi comes with a thermometer probe that is inserted into the center of a seasoned steak, to alert you when it's reached your desire doneness. Once the internal temperature of the steak reaches that temperature, you open the lid and have the perfectly cooked dinner. It really is that easy! Alongside your steak, you can also enjoy perfectly roasted vegetables and potatoes, and you can even enjoy a fresh-baked apple pie for dessert... all from your Ninja Foodi!

One of the finest parts of this machine though is that it reaches a temperature of 500F – this is almost unheard of for a tabletop interior grill. This high temperature allows me to properly sear my food (especially steaks, chicken, or fish) and really allows it to get those tasty grill marks. But this device does more than just sear, as I've told you... because of its unique cyclonic technology, it also circulates the air around your food continuously, which cooks food perfectly, every time.

Ninja Foodi Smart XL Grill

Characteristics	Ninja Foodi AG301 Grill	Ninja Foodi Smart XL Grill
Cooking programs	There are five cook programs. Grill, Air crisp, Bake, Roast, and Dehydrate.	There are six cook programs. Broil, Dehydrate, Air crisp, Roast, Bake, and Grill.
Smart temperature probe	Absent. You have to rely a bit on guesswork to attain that perfect doneness.	Dual sensor Present. To continuously monitor the temperature accuracy for even more perfect doneness. Multi-task away since it cancels the need to watch over the food.
Smart cook system	Absent. Requires frequent checks and guesswork for satisfactory results.	Present. With 4 smart protein settings and 9 customizable doneness levels, all the work is done to input the required setting. Just wait for your food to cook. You could be busy doing your laundry while you cook.
Weight	20 pounds	27.5 pounds
Dimension (L×W×H) inches	12.5 ×16.88×10.59 inches.	18.8 x 17.7 x 14 inches. Therefore, this is the larger option for large-sized family dishes and 50% more grilling space.

CHAPTER 2:

Breakfast Recipes

1. Supreme Garlic Potatoes

Preparation Time: 10 minutes

Cooking Time 20 minutes

Servings:: 4

Ingredients:

- 2 pounds baby red potatoes, quartered

- 2 tablespoons extra virgin olive oil

- 1/4 cup dried onion flakes

- 1/2 teaspoon onion powder

- 1/2 teaspoon garlic powder

- 1/4 teaspoon celery powder

- 1/4 teaspoon freshly ground black pepper

- 1/2 teaspoon dried parsley

- 1/2 teaspoon salt

Directions:

1. Take a large bowl and add all listed ingredients, toss well and coat them well

2. Pre-heat Ninja Foodi by pressing the "AIR CRISP" option and setting it to "390 Degrees F" and timer to 20 minutes

3. let it pre-heat until you hear a beep

4. Once preheated, add potatoes to the cooking basket

5. Lock and cook for 10 minutes, making sure to shake the basket and cook for 10 minutes more

6. Once done, check the crispiness, if it's alright, serve away.

7. If not, cook for 5 minutes more

8. Enjoy!

Nutrition:

- Calories: 232 kcal

- Carbs: 39 g

- Fat: 7 g

- Protein: 4 g

2. Potato Pancakes

Preparation Time: 10 minutes

Cooking Time 24 minutes

Servings: 4

Ingredients:

- 4 medium potatoes, peeled and cleaned

- 1 medium onion, chopped

- 1 beaten egg

- 1/4 milk

- 2 tablespoons unsalted butter

- 1/2aspoon garlic powder

- 1/4aspoon salt

- 3 tablespoons all-purpose flour

- Pepper as needed

Directions:

1. Peel your potatoes and shred them up

2. Soak the shredded potatoes under cold water to remove starch

3. Drain the potatoes

4. Take a bowl and add eggs, milk, butter, garlic powder, salt, and pepper

5. Add in flour

6. Mix well

7. Add the shredded potatoes

8. Pre-heat Ninja Foodi by pressing the "AIR CRISP" option and setting it to "390 Degrees F" and timer to 24 minutes

9. let it pre-heat until you hear a beep

10. Add ¼ cup of the potato pancake batter to your cooking basket and cook for 12 minutes until the golden-brown texture is seen

11. Enjoy!

Nutrition:

- Calories: 240 kcal

- Carbs: 33 g

- Fat: 11 g

- Protein: 6 g

3. Sausage and Cheese Wraps

Preparation: 5 minutes **Cooking time:** 8 minutes **Servings:** 4

Ingredients:

- 2 pieces American cheese, cut into quarters

- 1 (8 counts) can crescent roll dough, refrigerated

- Ketchup dipping 8 Jimmy Dean® Heat n' serve sausages

Directions:

1. Select the GRILL button on the Ninja Foodi Smart XL Grill and regulate at MED for 10 minutes.

2. Put the sausage and cheese over the crescent rolls.

3. Bind the sausages inside the rolls and seal the edges.

4. Arrange the rolls in the Ninja Foodi when it displays ADD FOOD. Grill for 8 minutes, flipping once in between.

5. Dole out on a platter and serve with some ketchup dripping.

Nutrition:

- Calories: 331 Fat: 2.5 g. Sat Fat: 0.5 g.

- Carbohydrates: 69 g. Fiber: 12.2 g. Sugar: 8.1 g.

- Protein: 8.7 g.

4. Honey Glazed Ham

Preparation time: 20 minutes.

Cooking time: 1 hour 15 minutes.

Servings: 15

Ingredients:

- 1(5 pounds) ready-to-eat ham

- ¼ cup of whole cloves

- ¼ cup of dark corn syrup

- 2 cups of honey

- 2/3 Cup of butter

Directions:

- Preheat Ninja Foodi Smart XL by pressing the "bake" set to 165°C (325°F).

- Rate a ham and a stud with all the cloves. Put the ham in a pan lined with foil.

- Heat the corn syrup, honey and butter in the top half of a double boiler. Keep the glaze warm when the ham is baking.

- Glaze over the ham and then bake in the preheated Ninja Foodi for 1 hour and 15 minutes. Baste the ham with a honey glaze every 10 to 15 minutes. Turn on the broiler to caramelize the ice during the last 4 to 5 minutes of baking. Remove from the Ninja Foodi smart and leave to rest before serving for a few minutes.

Nutrition:

- Energy (calories): 836

- Protein: 9.88g

- Fat: 9.11g

- Carbohydrates: 177.47g

5. Black Bean and Corn Couscous Salad (Cold Soak)Errore. Il segnalibro non è definito.

Preparation time: 25 minutes.

Cooking time: 5 minutes.

Servings: 4

Ingredients:

- 1(½) cups water

- 3 tablespoons oil, divided

- ½ teaspoon salt

- 1 cup couscous

- Freshly squeezed juice from 3 limes

- 2 tablespoons rice vinegar

- ½ teaspoon ground cumin

- ¼ cup minced fresh cilantro

- ½ cup fresh cheese, finely crumbled (optional)

- 1 (15-ounce) can Dark beans

- 1 cup Corn

- 2 cups of diced Zucchini

- 1 tablespoon of Bean stew powder

To pack for the trail:

- ½ cup roasted and salted pepitas (pumpkin seeds)

Directions:

1. In a medium pot, add the water, 1 tablespoon of oil, and the salt and heat to the point of boiling. Remove the pot from the warmth, include the couscous, and mix to blend. Spread the pot and let it sit for 5 minutes. Lighten the couscous with a fork and move it to a huge bowl.

2. In a little bowl, blend the remaining 2 tablespoons of oil, lime juice, rice vinegar, cumin, bean stew powder, and dark pepper. Put the dressing in a safe spot.

3. Put the dark beans, corn, zucchini, and cilantro in the bowl containing the couscous. Mix to blend, at that point, add the dressing and Cheddar (if utilizing). Mix well.

4. **To dehydrate:** Spread the serving of mixed greens out equitably on the dehydrator plate fitted with a strong plastic addition. Put the plate in the Ninja Foodi Smart XL. Set to 135°F for 6 hours. At the 6-hour mark, check the vegetables.

The zucchini and beans ought to be hard to the touch and ought not to feel damp. In case it is important, continue drying the plate of mixed greens for another 1 to 2 hours.

5. **To store:** Measure the aggregate sum of serving of mixed greens, isolate it into four segments, and put each component in a bubble in a sack. Gap the pepitas into four little zip-fixed bags and put one inside every serving of mixed greens pack. Mark and date the packs. Store for as long as one year.

6. **To rehydrate:** Evacuate the little pack of pepitas. Include ½ cup of cool water to the serving of mixed greens sack. Blend it well, spread, and let it sit for 15 to 20 minutes. Mix the plate of mixed greens once more and sprinkle the pepitas over the top before eating.

Nutrition:

- **Calories:** 530 **Fat:** 23g
- **Carb:** 65g **Protein:** 22g **Sodium:** 680mg

CHAPTER 3:

Meat Recipes

6. Mozzarella Meatball Sandwiches with Basil

Preparation time: 5 minutes

Cooking time: 10 minutes

Servings: 4

Ingredients:

- 12 frozen meatballs

- 8 slices Mozzarella cheese

- 4 sub rolls, halved lengthwise

- ½ cup marinara sauce, warmed

- 12 fresh basil leaves

Directions:

1. Pullout the Crisper Basket and adjust the hood. Choice AIR CRISP set the temperature to 350°F (177°C) and set the time to 10 minutes. Select START/STOP to begin preheating.

2. When the unit toots to indicate it has preheated, place the meatballs in the basket. Close the hood and AIR CRISP for 5 minutes.

3. After 5 minutes, shake the basket of meatballs. Place the basket back in the unit and adjust the hood to resume cooking.

4. While the meatballs are cooking, place two slices of Mozzarella cheese on each sub roll. Use a spoon to spread the marinara sauce on top of the cheese slices. Press three leaves of basil into the sauce on each roll.

5. When cooking is complete, place three meatballs on each sub roll. Serve immediately.

Nutrition:

- Calories: 736

- Total fat: 48 g

- Saturated fat: 20 g

- Cholesterol: 198 mg

- Sodium: 974 mg

- Carbohydrates: 13 g

- Fiber: 3 g

- Protein: 61 g

7. Steak with Salsa Verde

Preparation time: 10 minutes

Cooking time: 18 minutes

Servings: 4

Ingredients:

- 2 beef flank steak, diced
- 2 cups salsa Verde
- 2 ripe avocados, diced
- 1 cup fresh cilantro leaves
- 2 medium tomatoes, seeded and diced
- 8 bread slices
- 1/2 tsp. salt
- 1/2 tsp. pepper

Directions:

1. Rub the steak with salt and pepper to season well.

2. Pre-heat Ninja Foodi by demanding the GRILL option and setting it to HIGH.

3. Once it pre-heat until you hear a beep, open the lid.

4. Place the bread slices on the grill.

5. Cover the lid and cook for 9 minutes.

6. Flip it and cook for 9 minutes more.

7. Blend salsa with cilantro in a blender, slice the steak and serve

   with salsa, tomato, and avocado.

8. Serve and enjoy!

Nutrition:

- Calories: 545

- Carbohydrates: 15 g.

- Fat: 36.4 g.

- Protein: 42.5 g.

8. Broiled Boneless Pork Chops

Preparation time: 10 minutes.

Cooking time: 10 minutes.

Servings: 4

Ingredients:

- 4 pork chops, boneless ¾ inch thick

- 1 tablespoon olive oil

- 1 tablespoon salt

- ½ tablespoon paprika

- Black pepper to taste

- 4 tablespoons pesto

- 4 slices of mozzarella cheese

- 1 thinly sliced tomato

Direction:

- Cut the pork chops down in the middle to form a flap.

- Rub the pork with olive oil, salt, paprika, and black pepper.

- Fill each of the pork chops with 1 tablespoon of pesto, a slice of mozzarella cheese, and three pieces of tomatoes.

- Place the pork chops on a baking tray.

- Set the temperature Ninja Foodi Smart XL Grill to broil setting.

- Rotate the timer knob to dark and broil the pork chops for 20 minutes at 450°F.

- Get the pork chops to a serving platter.

- Serve and enjoy.

Serving suggestions: serve these pork chops with lemon wedges.

Variation tip: mozzarella cheese can be replaced with favourite cheese.

Nutrition:

- **Calories:** 387

- **Protein:** 36g

- **Fat:** 24g

- **Carbs:** 3g

9. Broiled Rosemary Lamb Chops

Preparation time: 10 minutes.

Cooking time: 25 minutes.

Servings: 4

Ingredients:

- 6 lamb chops

- 3 tablespoons olive oil

- 2 tablespoons sea salt

- ½ tablespoon black peppercorns

- 4 garlic cloves cut in half

- 12 spring's fresh rosemary

Direction:

- In a mixing bowl, add lamb chops and then rub it with oil, salt, and pepper.

- Place the chops on a greased baking pan. Stick the garlic cloves into the chops.

- Roll rosemary springs between your hands to release the oil, and then place them on both sides of the chops.

- Place the baking pan on the rack in the upper position of the Ninja Foodi Smart XL Grill.

- Set the temperature to broil setting at 450°F.

- Broil for 10 minutes or until the internal smart temperature reaches 125°F. Let the chops cool before serving.

Serving suggestions: serve with your choice of sautéed veggies.

Variation tip: use avocado oil in place of olive oil.

Nutrition:

- Calories: 220

- Protein: 16g

- Fat: 16g

- Carbs: 2g

10.   Grilled Chicken with Lemon and Thyme Recipe

Preparation Time: 1 hour 30 Minutes

Cooking Time: 15-20 Minutes

Servings: 4

Ingredients:

- 3 tbsp. Plus 1/2 cup extra-virgin olive oils, divided, plus more for a grill

- 4 skin-on, bone-in chicken breasts (about 3 lb.)

- Kosher salt, freshly ground pepper

- 2 lemons

- 4 garlic cloves, crushed

- 3 large sprigs of thyme

- 1 cup torn pitted Castelvetrano olives

Directions:

1. Preheat the Ninja Foodi Smart XL. Select Grill, set the temperature to Medium, and set the time to 10 minutes. Select Start/stop to begin preheating.

2. Lightly oil grate. Pat chicken breasts dry; season generously around with salt and pepper. Place on baking sheet; let sit at room temperature for at least 30 minutes and up to at least one 1 hour.

3. Thinly slice one lemon crosswise into rounds; pluck out seeds. Put a half cut of the lemon slices in a little bowl. Add garlic and 1 tbsp. oil and mix to coat; season with salt and pepper. Set remaining lemon slices aside for serving. Slice remaining lemon in two and squeeze juice into another normal-sized bowl (you ought to have about 1/4 cup). Reserve.

4. Pat chicken dry again (the salt will have slow more moisture) and rub with 2 tbsp. oil. Grill oiled lemon slices over the hot side of the grill, about 3 minutes. Transfer to a plate. Grill chicken on the cooler side of the grill for 15-20 minutes. Grill until an instant-read thermometer is inserted into the thickest part of the breast registers 160°, 8-10 minutes longer.

5. Place chicken into a cutting board and let it rest 10-15 minutes.

6. Pull the chicken meat from bones and slice 1/2" thick. Put on a rimmed platter, shingling slices. Scatter thyme sprigs, olives,

grilled lemon slices, and reserved fresh lemon slices over. Season with an increase of salt and pepper; drizzle reserved lemon juice and remaining 1/2 cup oil throughout. Let it sit for at least 15 minutes and up to at least one hour before serving.

Nutrition:

- Calories: 1494

- Protein: 0.56 g

- Fat: 167.16 g

- Carbohydrates: 4.75 g

11.   Chicken Hot BBQ

Preparation Time: 5-10 minutes

Cooking Time: 18 minutes

Servings: 4

Ingredients:

- 2 tablespoons honey

- 1 pound chicken drumsticks

- 1 tablespoon hot sauce

- 2 cups barbecue sauce

- 1 lime juice

- Black pepper and sea salt to taste

Directions:

1. In a mixing bowl, add the barbecue sauce, lime juice, honey, pepper, salt, and hot sauce. Combine and set aside.

2. In a mixing bowl, add the ½ cup of the sauce and chicken. Combine the ingredients to mix well with each other.

3. Refrigerate for 1 hour to marinate.

4. Take Ninja Foodi Smart XL grill, put it over your kitchen platform, and open the top lid.

5. Place the grill grate and close the top lid.

6. Press "Grill" and select the "Medium" grill function. Adjust the timer to 18 minutes and then press "Start/stop." Ninja Foodi will start pre-heating.

7. Ninja Foodi Smart XL is preheated and ready to cook when it beeps. Open the top lid.

8. Arrange the chicken over the grill grate.

9. Close the top lid and allow cooking until the timer reads zero. Cook until the food thermometer reaches 165 °F.

10. Serve warm.

Nutrition:

*   Calories: 423

*   Fat: 13.5 g

*   Carbohydrates: 47.5 g

*   Fibre: 4 g

*   Protein: 22 g

12. Perfect grilled Pork Chops with Sweet BBQ Rub

Preparation Time: 10 Minutes

Cooking Time: 5-6 Minutes

Servings: 8

Ingredients:

- Four bone-in, thick center-cut or rib chops pork chops

- 2 tbsp. olive oil

Sweet BBQ Pork Rub:

- 1/4 tsp. onion powder

- 1/2 tsp. chilli powder

- 2 tsp. kosher salt

- 1 tsp. freshly ground black pepper

- 1/4 tsp. dried oregano

- 1/4 tsp. garlic powder

- 1 tsp. paprika 2 tbsp. Brown sugar

Directions:

1. Combine all of the rubbing ingredients in a small bowl and set aside.

2. Preheat the Ninja Foo Smart XL grill over Medium-high heat for 10 minutes around 400 °F.

3. Rub the pork chops using olive oil, and then sprinkle generously with the sweet barbecue sauce, rubbing the meat.

4. Arrange the pork chops on the grill over direct heat and brown for 4-6 minutes.

5. Move the pork chops to the grill's indirect heat side and cook for another 5-6 minutes until the smart thermometer reads 145 °F.

6. Get the pork chops from the grill and let them rest for 3 to 5 minutes before serving.

Nutrition:

- Calories: 236

- Protein: 32.42 g

- Fat: 10.58 g

- Carbohydrates: 0.8 g

CHAPTER 4:

Fish Recipes

13.   Juicy Lemon and Mustard Fish

Preparation time: 5-10 minutes

Cooking time: 10 minutes

Servings: 4

Ingredients:

- 2 fish fillets

- Salt and pepper to taste

- ½ teaspoon ground thyme

- 2 garlic cloves, minced

- 2 tablespoons olive oil

- 1 tablespoon Dijon mustard

- 2 tablespoons lemon juice

Directions:

1. Take a bowl and add listed ingredients, mix well.

2. Spread the mixture on top of the fish and the sides.

3. Add salmon to the crisping tray.

4. Transfer crisping tray to your Ninja Foodi Smart XL, set to AIR CRISP mode.

5. Air Fry for 7-10 minutes at 400 degrees F.

6. Serve and enjoy once done!

Nutrition:

- Calories: 341

- Fat: 15 g

- Saturated Fat: 5 g

- Carbohydrates: 3 g

- Fiber: 1 g

- Sodium: 372 mg

- Protein: 47 g

14.   Oriental Red Snapper

Preparation time: 10 minutes

Cooking time: 12 minutes

Servings:

Ingredients:

- 1 tbsp. lemon juice

- 2 lbs. red snapper fillets, boneless

- 3 garlic cloves, grated

- 1 tbsp. tamarind paste

- 1 yellow onion, chopped

- 1 tbsp. oriental sesame oil

- 2 tbsp. water

- 1 tbsp. grated ginger

- 1/2 tsp. ground cumin

- Salt and black pepper as desired

- 3 tbsp. chopped mint

Directions:

1. Place the cooking pot into the Ninja Foodi AG301, and position the grill plate with the handles facing up.

2. Ensure the splatter shield is in position. Close the lid.

3. Press the GRILL button. Set the temperature to 320°F and adjust the time to 12 minutes. Press the START/STOP button to preheat the appliance for 8 minutes.

4. Blend the water, garlic, ginger, cumin, sesame oil, tamarind paste, pepper, salt, and onion with a food processor.

5. Covering the fish with the blended mixture and transfer to the grill plate.

6. Close the lid.

7. Serve immediately

Serving suggestions: Drizzle fish with lemon and top with mint.

Preparation and cooking tips: Flip the items on the grill plate halfway.

Nutrition:

- Calories: 241

- Fat: 8 g.

- Carb: 17 g.

- Proteins: 12 g.

CHAPTER 5:

Vegetable Recipes

15.   Simple Pesto Gnocchi

Preparation time: 10 minutes

Cooking time: 15 minutes

Servings: 4

Ingredients:

- 1 (1-pound / 454-g) package gnocchi

- 1 medium onion, chopped

- 3 cloves garlic, minced

- 1 tablespoon extra-virgin olive oil

- 1 (8-ounce / 227-g) jar pesto

- 1/3 cup grated Parmesan cheese

Directions:

1. Insert the Crisper Basket and close the hood. Select AIR CRISP, set the temperature to 340°F (171°C), and set the time to 15 minutes. Select START/STOP to begin preheating.

2. In a large bowl combine the onion, garlic, and gnocchi, and drizzle with the olive oil. Mix thoroughly.

3. Transfer the mixture to the basket. Close the hood and AIR CRISP for 15 minutes, stirring occasionally, making sure the gnocchi become light brown and crispy.

4. Add the pesto and Parmesan cheese and give everything a good stir before serving.

Nutrition:

- Calories: 200

- Fat: 12 g

- Carb: 16 g

- Proteins: 15 g

16. Sesame-Thyme Whole Maitake Mushrooms

Preparation time: 5 minutes

Cooking time: 15 minutes

Servings: 2

Ingredients:

- 1 tbsp. soy sauce

- 2 tsp. toasted sesame oil

- 3 tsp. vegetable oil, divided

- 1 garlic clove, minced

- 7 oz. (198 g.) Maitake mushrooms

- 1/2 tsp. flaky sea salt

- 1/2 tsp. sesame seeds

- 1/2 tsp. fresh thyme leaves, finely chopped

Directions:

1. Insert the Crisper Basket and close the lid. Select ROAST, set the temperature to 300°F (149°C), and set the time to 15 minutes. Use START/STOP to preheat.

2. Whisk together the soy sauce, sesame oil, 1 tsp. of vegetable oil, and garlic in a small bowl.

3. Arrange the mushrooms in the Crisper Basket in a single layer. Drizzle the soy sauce mixture over the mushrooms. Close the lid and ROAST for 10 minutes.

4. Flip the mushrooms and sprinkle the sea salt, sesame seeds, and thyme leaves on top. Drizzle the remaining 2 tsp. of vegetable oil all over. Roast for an additional 5 minutes.

5. Remove the mushrooms from the basket to a plate and serve hot.

Nutrition:

- Calories: 400

- Fat: 20 g.

- Saturated Fat: 10 g.

- Carbohydrates: 36 g.

- Fiber: 5 g.

- Sodium: 675 mg.

- Protein: 22 g.

17.   Baked Lemon Broccoli

Preparation time: 10 minutes.

Cooking time: 35 minutes.

Servings: 4

Ingredients:

- 1(1/2) pounds broccoli florets

- 1/2 teaspoon garlic powder

- 2(1/2) tablespoon olive oil

- 1 tablespoon fresh lemon juice

- 1/4 teaspoon onion powder

- 1/4 teaspoon pepper

- 1/2 teaspoon salt

Directions:

- In a bowl, toss broccoli with onion powder, garlic powder, olive oil, pepper, and salt.

- Place the cooking pot in the unit, then close the hood.

- Select bake mode and then set the temperature to 390°F and set the timer to 25 minutes. Press start to begin preheating.

- Once the unit is preheated, it will beep, then place broccoli florets in the cooking pot. Close the hood.

- Cook broccoli for 25 minutes or until tender.

- Drizzle lemon juice over broccoli and serve.

Nutrition:

- **Calories:** 134

- **Fat:** 9.3g

- **Carbohydrates:** 11.8g

- **Sugar:** 3g

- **Protein:** 5g

- **Cholesterol:** 0mg

18. Dehydrated Potatoes Sticks

Preparation: 5 minutes. **Cooking time:** 2 hours. **Servings:** 4

Ingredients:

- 2 large potatoes, peeled and cut into thin slices like a matchstick

Directions

1. Peel the potatoes and cut them into skinny shapes like a matchstick. You can use an automatic round potato chip cutting machine to make the job done.

2. Layer the round chips on to the dehydrating rack and place the rack inside the Ninja Foodi.

3. Turn on the Ninja Foodi Smart XL Grill by pressing the dehydrator option and set the temperature to 195°F.

4. Set time to 2 hours.

5. Take out and serve.

Nutrition:

- **Calories:** 255 **Fat:** 0.4g **Cholesterol:** 0mg

- **Sodium:** 22mg **Carbohydrate:** 58g **Dietary fiber:** 8.9g

- **Protein:** 6.2g

19.   Dehydrated Plum Tomatoes

Preparation time: 2 minutes

Cooking time: 9 hours

Servings: 2

Ingredients:

- 2 plum tomatoes

- 4 pinches of salt

Directions:

1. Slice the plum tomatoes in half and then scrape out the seeds.

2. Now make a shallow slit into the skin.

3. Sprinkle some salt. Drain any excess liquid.

4. Layer the plum tomatoes on the dehydrating racks and place the rack inside the Ninja Foodi.

5. Set temperature to 135°F to 140°F for 9 hours.

6. Once done, take out.

Nutrition:

- **Calories:** 57 **Fat:** 0.5g **holesterol:** 0mg

- **Carbohydrate:** 12.6g **Dietary fiber:** 2.7g

- **Protein:** 3g

20.   Dehydrated Clementine's

Preparation time: 8 minutes.

Cooking time: 6 hours.

Servings: 2

Ingredients

- 2 Clementine's, peeled

- Salt and black pepper, to taste

Directions

1. The first step is to peel the Clementine's and slices, then road very thinly.

2. You can keep the peel intake if you like the flavour.

3. Sprinkle salt and black pepper on slices as per liking.

4. Layer the slices on the dehydrating rack.

5. Put the dehydrate rack inside the Ninja Foodi Smart XL Grill

6. Turn on the Ninja Foodi, press the dehydrate button, set the temperature to 135°F, and set the time to 6 hours.

7. Once cooking time completes, turn off the Ninja Foodi Smart XL.

8. Open the unit and take out the spicy and tangy Clementine jerky.

9. Serve once cool down.

Nutrition

- **Calories:** 35

- **Fat:** 0.1g

- **Saturated fat:** 0g

- **Cholesterol:** 0mg

- **Carbohydrate:** 8.9g

- **Dietary fiber:** 1.3g

- **Protein.** 0.6g

CHAPTER 6:

Appetizers and Snacks Recipes

21.   Seasoned Broccoli Dish

Preparation time: 10 minutes

Cooking time: 10 minutes

Servings: 4

Ingredients:

- 1-pound broccoli, cut into florets

- 1/4 teaspoon turmeric powder

- 1 tablespoon chickpea flour

- 2 tablespoons yogurt

- 1/4 teaspoon spice mix

- 1/2 teaspoon red chili powder

- 1/2 teaspoon salt

Directions:

1. Wash the broccoli florets thoroughly.

2. Take a bowl. Add all ingredients except florets. Mix well.

3. Add florets to the mix and let them sit in the fridge for 30 minutes.

4. Take your Ninja Foodi Smart XL Grill and open the lid, arrange the grill grate, and close the top.

5. Pre-heat Ninja Foodi. Press the "AIR CRISP" option and set it to "390 Degrees F and timer to 10 min.

6. Arrange florets over the Grill Basket and lock lid, cook for 10 minutes.

7. Serve and enjoy!

Nutrition:

- Calories: 113

- Carbs: 12 g

- Fat: 2 g

- Protein: 0.7 g

22. Simple Crispy Brussels

Preparation time: 10 minutes

Cooking time: 12 minutes

Servings: 4

Ingredients:

- 1-pound Brussels sprouts, halved   2 tablespoons olive oil, extra virgin 1/2 teaspoon ground black pepper

- 1 teaspoon salt 6 slices bacon, chopped

Directions:

1. Take a mixing bowl and add Brussels, olive oil, salt, pepper, and bacon

2. Pre-heat Ninja Foodi. Press the "AIR CRISP" option and set it to "390 degrees F" and the timer to 12 min.

3. Arrange Brussels over basket and lock lid, cook for 6 minutes, shake, and cook for 6 minutes more

4. Serve and enjoy!

Nutrition:

- Calories: 279 Carbs: 12 g Fat: 18 g Protein: 14 g

23.   The Noble Family Lemon Mousse

Preparation: 10 minutes **Cooking:** 12 minutes **Servings:** 4

Ingredients:

- 1–2 oz. cream cheese, soft 1/2 cup heavy cream

- 1/8 cup fresh lemon juice 1/2 tsp. lemon liquid stevia

- 2 pinch salt

Directions:

1. Take a bowl and mix in cream cheese, heavy cream, lemon juice, salt, and stevia.

2. Pour mixture into a ramekin and transfer to Ninja Foodi.

3. Lock the lid and choose the BAKE/ROAST mode and bake for 12 minutes at 350°F.

4. Check using a toothpick if it comes out clean. Serve and enjoy!

Nutrition:

- Calories: 225 Fat: 17 g. Saturated Fat: 5 g.

- Carbohydrates: 13 g. Fiber: 3 g. Sodium: 284 mg.

- Protein: 6 g.

.

CHAPTER 7:

Desserts Recipes

24.   Spice Lover's Cajun Eggplant

Preparation time: 5-10 minutes

Cooking time: 12 minutes

Servings: 4

Ingredients:

- 2 small eggplants, cut into slices

- 3 tsp. Cajun seasoning

- 1/4 cup olive oil

- 2 tbsp. lime juice

Directions:

1. Coat eggplant slices with oil, lime juice, and Cajun seasoning in a mixing bowl.

2. Take your Ninja Foodi Smart XL Grill and press GRILL, and set it to MED mode.

3. Set the timer to 10 minutes.

4. Let it preheat until you hear a beep.

5. Arrange eggplants over the grill grate and lock the lid.

6. Cook for 5 minutes.

7. Flip and cook for 5 minutes more.

8. Serve and enjoy!

Nutrition:

- Calories: 362

- Fat: 11 g.

- Saturated Fat: 3 g.

- Carbohydrates: 16 g.

- Fiber: 1 g.

- Sodium: 694 mg.

- Protein: 8 g.

25.   Curry Peaches, Pears, and Plums

Preparation time: 5 minutes.

Cooking time: 5 minutes.

Servings: 6–8

Ingredients:

- 2 peaches

- 2 firm pears

- 2 plums

- 2 tablespoons melted butter

- 1 tablespoon honey

- 2 to 3 teaspoons curry powder

Directions:

- Insert the Crisper Basket and close the hood. Select bake, set the temperature to 325°F (163°C) and set the time to 8 minutes. Select start/stop to begin preheating.

- Cut the peaches in half, and then remove the pits, and cut each half in half again. Cut the pears in half, clean them, and remove the stem. Cut each half in half as well. Do the same with the plums.

- Place a large sheet of heavy-duty foil on the work surface. Arrange the fruit on the foil and pour butter and honey. Sprinkle with curry powder.

- Wrap the fruit in the foil, making sure to leave some air space in the packet.

- Put the foil package in the basket. Close the hood and bake for 5 to 8 minutes, shaking the basket once during the cooking time, until the fruit is soft.

- Serve immediately.

Nutrition:

- **Energy (calories):** 52

- **Protein:** 0.17g

- **Fat:** 3.38g

- **Carbohydrates:** 5.85g

26.   Apple, Peach, and Cranberry Crisp

Preparation time: 10 minutes.

Cooking time: 12 minutes.

Servings: 8

Ingredients:

- 1 apple, peeled and chopped

- 2 peaches, peeled and chopped

- 1/3 cup dried cranberries

- 2 tablespoons honey

- 1/3 cup brown sugar

- ¼ cup flour

- ½ cup oatmeal

- 3 tablespoons softened butter

Directions:

- Select bake, set the temperature to 370°F (188°C) and set the time to 12 minutes. Select start/stop to begin preheating.

- In a baking pan, combine the apple, peaches, cranberries, honey, and mix well.

- In a medium bowl, combine the brown sugar, flour, oatmeal, and butter, and mix until crumbly. Sprinkle the mixture to the fruit in a pan.

- Place the pan directly in the pot. Close the hood and bake for 10 to 12 minutes or until the fruit is bubbly, and the topping is golden brown. Serve warm.

Nutrition:

- Energy (calories): 213

- Fat: 4.58g

- Carbohydrates: 44.09g

CHAPTER 8:

Main Recipes

27. Crispy Air Fryer Chickpeas

Preparation time: 10 minutes

Cooking time: 15 Minutes

Servings: 3

Ingredients:

- 16 ounces of chickpeas, drained and rinsed

- 1 tablespoon olive oil

- 1-ounce packet ranch salad dressing & seasoning mix

- 3 tablespoons parmesan cheese

Directions:

1. Heat the Ninja Foodi air fryer at 390 degrees for 10 minutes.

2. Ditch and wash the chickpeas in a bowl, and then toss in one tablespoon of olive oil.

3. Toss parmesan cheese and ranch seasoning as well.

4. Mix all the ingredients well.

5. Now pour the chicken peas into the air fryer basket.

6. Let it cook for 15 minutes.

7. Remember to shake the chickpeas in between.

8. When the chickpeas are crisp, remove them from the basket.

9. Store in an airtight container or service.

10. Enjoy.

Nutrition:

- Calories 190

% Daily Value*

- Total Fat 13.6 g 17%

- Saturated Fat 3.4 g 17%

- Cholesterol 327 mg 109%

- Sodium 126 mg 5%

- Total Carbohydrate 6.2 g 2%

- Dietary Fiber 2 g 7%

- Total Sugars 3.5 g

- Protein 12.1 g

28.   Easy Carne Asada Tacos

Preparation time: 15 minutes.

Cooking time: 15 minutes.

Servings: 4 to 6.

Ingredients:

- 2 tablespoons soy sauce

- Juice of 2 limes

- 2 tablespoons avocado oil, divided

- 4 garlic cloves, minced

- 2 teaspoons chilli powder

- 1 teaspoon ground cumin

- ½ teaspoon salt

- ¼ teaspoon freshly ground black pepper

- 1(½) pounds (680 grams) skirt steak or flank steak

- 12 corn tortillas 1 small red onion, diced

- 1 jalapeno, sliced ½ cup chopped fresh cilantro

Directions:

- In a prepared medium bowl, whisk together the soy sauce, lime juice, avocado oil, garlic, chili powder, cumin, salt, and pepper. Pour the marinade into a compatible resealable bag, then add the steak, seal the bag, and you can marinate in the refrigerator for 1 hour.

- Get the steak from the marinade and place it in the center of the sheet pan.

- Install a wire rack on Level 4. Select broil and set the temperature to HI and set the time to 15 minutes. Press start/stop to begin. Place the Ninja pan inside and close the door to start cooking.

- When cooking is complete, transfer the steak to a cutting board and let it cool for 10 minutes before slicing.

- Divide the sliced steak among the tortillas, then topping with the onion, jalapeno, and cilantro.

Nutrition:

- **Energy (calories):** 265

- **Protein:** 30.16g

- **Fat:** 13.91g

- **Carbohydrates:** 3.64g

29.   Italian Parmesan Meatball Al Forno

Preparation time: 20 minutes.

Cooking time: 35 minutes.

Servings: 6 to 8.

Ingredients:

- ½ cup Italian-style breadcrumbs

- ¼ cup whole milk

- 2 pounds (907 grams) ground meatloaf mix (ground beef, pork, and veal)

- 1(½) cups grated Parmesan cheese, divided

- 2 large eggs, beaten

- 1 teaspoon garlic powder

- 1 teaspoon red pepper flakes

- 1 tablespoon Italian seasoning

- Kosher salt and some freshly ground black pepper to taste

- 1(24-ounce/680 grams) jar marinara sauce

- ½ cup beef stock

- 8 ounces (227 grams) mozzarella cheese

- Fresh basil leaves, torn for garnish

Directions:

- In a prepared large bowl, stir together the breadcrumbs and milk and let it sit for 5 minutes.

- After the breadcrumbs and milk have sat for 5 minutes, add the meatloaf mix, ¾ cup of Parmesan, the eggs, garlic powder, red pepper flakes, Italian seasoning, salt, and pepper to the bowl. Mix well to combine thoroughly.

- Using a ¼-cup measure, fill it with the meatloaf mixture and then roll it into balls. Place the meatballs on the roast tray nested in a sheet pan.

- Install a wire rack. Select roast, set the temperature to 400°F (204°C) and set 30 minutes. Press start/stop to begin preheating.

- When the unit has preheated, place the sheet pan and roast tray on the wire rack. Close the oven door to begin cooking.

- Meanwhile, combine the marinara sauce and beef stock in the casserole dish.

- After 15 minutes, remove the sheet pan and roast tray from the oven and place the meatballs, browned-side down, in the sauce in the casserole dish. Place the casserole dish on the wire rack and continue cooking.

- When cooking is complete, remove the dish and sprinkle the meatballs with the Mozzarella and the remaining ½ cup of Parmesan.

- Select Broil, set the temperature to HI, and set the time to 5 minutes. Press Start/Stop to begin.

- Place the casserole dish on the wire rack and broil until the cheese is melted and starting to brown. Garnish with the basil before serving.

Nutrition:

- **Energy (calories):** 413

- **Protein:** 27.73g

- **Fat:** 28.67g

Carbohydrates: 9.88g

30.   Sun-Dried Tomatoes

Preparation time: 5 minutes.

Cooking time: 2 hours.

Servings: 4

Ingredients:

- 1-pound fresh red tomatoes halved

Directions:

1. Press the power button on the Ninja Foodi Grill. Select the dehydrate setting.

2. Press the start button and place the grill tray.

3. Place the tomatoes on the grill tray.

4. Adjust the cooking time to 2 hours and the temperature to 130°F.

5. Store in airtight containers until ready to consume.

Nutrition:

- **Calories:** 30 **Fat:** 0.3g

- **Carbs:** 4g **Protein:** 1g

- **Fiber:** 2g

31. Dehydrated Banana Chips

Preparation time: 5 minutes.

Cooking time: 2 hours.**Servings:** 4

Ingredients:

- 4 ripe bananas, peeled and sliced

- 2 teaspoon olive oil

Directions:

1. Press the power button on the Ninja Foodi Smart XL Grill. Select the dehydrate setting.

2. Press the start button and place the grill tray.

3. Toss the bananas with olive oil.

4. Place bananas on the grill tray.

5. Adjust the cooking time to 2 hours and the temperature to 130°F. Store in airtight containers until ready to consume.

Nutrition:

- **Calories:** 328 **Fat:** 16g **Carbs:** 44g

- **Protein:** 2g **Fiber:** 5g

32.   Dehydrated Eggplant

Preparation time: 5 minutes.

Cooking time: 2 hours.

Servings: 4

Ingredients:

- 1 medium-sized eggplant sliced crosswise

- 1(½) teaspoon smoked paprika

- 1 teaspoon liquid smoke

- ¼ teaspoon garlic powder

- ¼ teaspoon onion powder

- 1 teaspoon nutritional yeast

Directions:

1. Put the eggplants with the rest of the ingredients.

2. Press the power button on the Ninja Foodi Smart XL Grill. Select the dehydrate setting.

3. Press the start button and place the grill tray.

4. Place seasoned eggplants on the grill tray.

5. Adjust the cooking time to 2 hours and the temperature to 130°F.

6.   Store in airtight containers until ready to consume.

Nutrition:

- **Calories:** 95.2

- **Fat:** 0.8g

- **Carbs:** 18g

- **Protein:** 4g

33.   Chipotle Tofu Jerky

Preparation time: 5 minutes.

Cooking time: 2 hours.

Servings: 4

Ingredients:

- 1 block extra-firm tofu, sliced

- 1 tablespoon smoked paprika

- 1 tablespoon nutritional yeast

- 1 teaspoon cumin

- ¼ teaspoon chipotle powder

- Salt and pepper to taste

Directions:

1. Toss all the ingredients in a bowl.

2. Press the power button on the Ninja Foodi Grill. Select the dehydrate setting.

3. Press the start button and place the grill tray.

4. Place seasoned tofu on the grill tray.

5. Adjust the cooking time to 2 hours and the temperature to 130°F.

6. Store in airtight containers until ready to consume.

Nutrition:

- **Calories:** 274

- **Fat:** 14g

- **Carbs:** 11g

- **Protein:** 26g

34.   Sriracha and Garlic Kale

Preparation time: 5 minutes.

Cooking time: 2 hours.

Servings: 4

Ingredients:

- 1 bunch kale leaves, washed and air dried

- 2 tablespoons nutritional yeast

- 1 tablespoon Sriracha powder

- ¼ teaspoon garlic powder

- 1 teaspoon coconut oil

- 2 tablespoons olive oil

Directions:

1. Toss all the ingredients in a bowl.

2. Press the power button on the Ninja Foodi Smart XL Grill. Select the dehydrate setting.

3. Press the start button.

4. Place seasoned kale leaves in the cooking pot

5. Adjust the cooking time to 2 hours and the temperature to 130°F.

6. Store in airtight containers until ready to consume.

Nutrition:

- **Calories:** 184

- **Fat:** 16g

- **Carbs:** 5g

- **Protein:** 5g

CHAPTER 9:

Sides Recipes

35.   Tofu Italian Style

Preparation time: 5 min

Cooking time: 6 min

Servings: 4

Ingredients:

- 1 tablespoon tamari

- 8 ounces extra-firm tofu, pressed and cubed

- 1 tablespoon aquafaba

- ½ teaspoon dried basil

- ¼ teaspoon onion, granulated

- ½ teaspoon dried oregano

- ½ teaspoon garlic, granulated

- Black pepper to taste

Directions:

1. Press the "Air Crisp" button on the Ninja Foodi Smart XL Grill and adjust the temperature to 400 degrees F for 6 minutes.

2. Combine the tofu with the remaining ingredients in a bowl and marinate for 20 minutes.

3. Put the tofu in the Ninja Foodi when it shows "Add Food."

4. Dish out the tofu when completely cooked and serve warm.

Nutrition:

- Calories: 248

- Fat: 2.4 g

- Saturated Fat: 0.1 g

- Trans Fat: 2.4 g

- Carbohydrates: 2.2 g

- Fiber: 0.7 g

- Sodium: 350 mg

- Protein: 44.3 g

CHAPTER 10:

Poultry Recipes

36.   Southern-Style Chicken

Preparation time: 5 minutes

Cooking time: 20 minutes

Servings: 6

Ingredients:

- 2 cups Ritz crackers, crushed

- 1 tablespoon fresh parsley, minced

- 1 teaspoon garlic salt

- ¼ teaspoon rubbed sage

- 1 teaspoon paprika

- 1 large egg, beaten

- ½ teaspoon black pepper

- 1 (3-4 pounds) broiler/fryer chicken, cut up

- ¼ teaspoon ground cumin

Directions:

1. Select the "Air Crisp" button on the Ninja Foodi Smart XL Grill and regulate the 350 degrees F settings for 20 minutes.

2. Whip the egg in a bowl and mingle the rest of the ingredients except chicken in another bowl.

3. Immerse the chicken in the whipped egg and then dredge in the dry mixture.

4. Arrange the chicken in the Ninja Foodi when it displays "Add Food".

5. Air crisp for about 20 minutes and dole out to serve warm.

Nutrition:

- Calories: 391

- Fat: 2.8 g

- Sat Fat: 0.6 g

- Carbohydrates: 16.5 g

- Fiber: 9.2 g

- Sugar: 4.2 g

- Protein: 26.6 g

37.   Herbed Roasted Chicken

Preparation: 5 minutes **Cooking time:** 18 minutes **Servings:** 4

Ingredients:

- Salt to taste 4 chicken thighs, skin on, bone removed

- Black pepper for garnish Garlic powder to taste

Directions:

1. Select the "Air Crisp" button on the Ninja Foodi Smart XL Grill and regulate the settings at 400 degrees F for 18 minutes.

2. Dust the chicken with garlic powder and salt.

3. Arrange the chicken in the Ninja Foodi when it displays "Add Food".

4. Air crisp for 18 minutes, flipping once in between.

5. Dole out in a platter and dust with black pepper to serve.

Nutrition:

- Calories: 140 Fat: 7.9 g Sat Fat: 1.8 g

- Carbohydrates: 2.6 g Fiber: 1.8 g

- Sugar: 1.5 g

- Protein: 7.2 g

38. Orange and Honey Glazed Duck with Apples

Preparation time: 5 minutes

Cooking time: 15 minutes

Servings: 2 to 3

Ingredients:

- 1-pound (454 g) duck breasts (2 to 3 breasts)

- Kosher salt and pepper, to taste

- Juice and zest of 1 orange

- ¼ cup honey

- 2 sprigs thyme, plus more for garnish

- 2 firm tart apples, such as Fuji

Ingredients:

1. Insert the Crisper Basket and close the hood. Select ROAST, set the temperature to 400°F (204°C), and set the time to 13 minutes. Select START/STOP to begin preheating.

2. Pat the duck breasts dry and, using a sharp knife, make 3 to 4 shallow, diagonal slashes in the skin. Turn the breasts and

score the skin on the diagonal in the opposite direction to create a crosshatch pattern. Season well with salt and pepper.

3. Place the duck breasts skin-side up in the Crisper Basket. Close the hood and ROAST for 8 minutes. Flip and roast for 4 more minutes on the second side.

4. While the duck is roasting, prepare the sauce. Combine the orange juice and zest, honey, and thyme in a small saucepan. Bring to a boil, stirring to dissolve the honey, then reduce the heat and simmer until thickened. Core the apples and cut them into quarters. Cut each quarter into 3 or 4 slices depending on the size.

5. After the duck has cooked on both sides, turn it, and brush the skin with the orange-honey glaze. Roast for 1 more minute. Remove the duck breasts to a cutting board and allow to rest.

6. Toss the apple slices with the remaining orange-honey sauce in a medium bowl. Arrange the apples in a single layer in the Crisper Basket. AIR CRISP for 10 minutes while the duck breast rests. Slice the duck breasts on the bias and divide them and the apples among 2 or 3 plates.

7. Serve warm, garnished with additional thyme.

Nutrition:

- Calories: 320

- Fat: 14 g

- Saturated Fat: 4 g

- Carbohydrates: 19 g

- Fiber: 1 g

- Sodium: 258 mg

- Protein: 25 g

39. Crispy Chicken Cutlets

Preparation Time: 5 minutes

Cooking Time: 11 minutes

Servings: 2

Ingredients:

- ½ pound boneless, skinless chicken breasts, horizontally sliced in half, into cutlets ½ tbsp. extra-virgin olive oil

- 1/8 cup bread crumbs

- ¼ tsp. sea salt

- ¼ tsp. freshly ground black pepper

- ¼ tsp. paprika

- ¼ tsp. garlic powder

- 1/8 tsp. onion powder

Directions:

1. Insert the Crisper Basket and close the hood. Select Air Crisp, set the temperature to 375 °F. and set the time to 11 minutes. Select Start/stop to begin preheating.

2. Brush both sides of the chicken cutlets with the oil.

3. Combine the bread crumbs, salt, pepper, paprika, garlic powder, and onion powder in a Medium shallow bowl. Dredge the chicken cutlets in the bread crumb mixture, turning several times to ensure the chicken is fully coated.

4. When the Ninja Foodi Smart XL beeps, it has preheated, then place the chicken in the basket. Close the hood and cook for 9 minutes. It is completed when the internal temperature of the meat reaches at least 165 °F. on a food thermometer. If needed, cook for up to 2 minutes more.

5. Remove the chicken cutlets and serve immediately.

Nutrition:

- Calories: 103

- Protein: 5.42 g

- Fat: 3.29 g

- Carbohydrates: 12.7 g

40.   The Ultimate Turkey Burger

Preparation Time: 5 minutes

Cooking Time: 13 minutes

Servings: 4

Ingredients:

- 1 pound ground turkey

- ½ red onion, minced

- 1 jalapeño pepper, seeded, stemmed, and minced

- 3 tbsp. Bread crumbs

- 1½ tsp. ground cumin 1 tsp. paprika

- ½ tsp. cayenne pepper ½ tsp. sea salt

- ½ tsp. freshly ground black pepper

- 4 burger buns, for serving

- Lettuce, tomato, and cheese, if desired, for serving

- Ketchup and mustard, if desired, for serving

Directions:

1. Put inside the grill grate and close the hood. Select grill, then set the temperature to High, and the time to 13 minutes. Select Start/stop to begin preheating.

2. In the meantime, in a prepared large bowl, use your hands to combine the ground turkey, red onion, jalapeño pepper, bread crumbs, cumin, paprika, cayenne pepper, salt, and black pepper. Mix until just combined; be careful not to overwork the burger mixture.

3. Dampen your hands with cool water and form the turkey mixture into four patties.

4. When the Ninja Foodi Smart XL beeps, it has preheated, then place the burgers on the grill grate. Close the hood and cook for 11 minutes.

5. After 11 minutes, check the burgers for doneness. It is completely cooked when the internal temperature reaches at least 165 °F. on a food thermometer. If necessary, close the hood and continue cooking for up to 2 minutes more.

6. Once the burgers are done, place each patty on a bun. Top with your preferred fixings, such as lettuce, tomato, cheese, ketchup, and mustard.

Nutrition:

- Calories: 652 Protein: 25.19 g Fat: 51.86 g Carbohydrates: 19.82 g

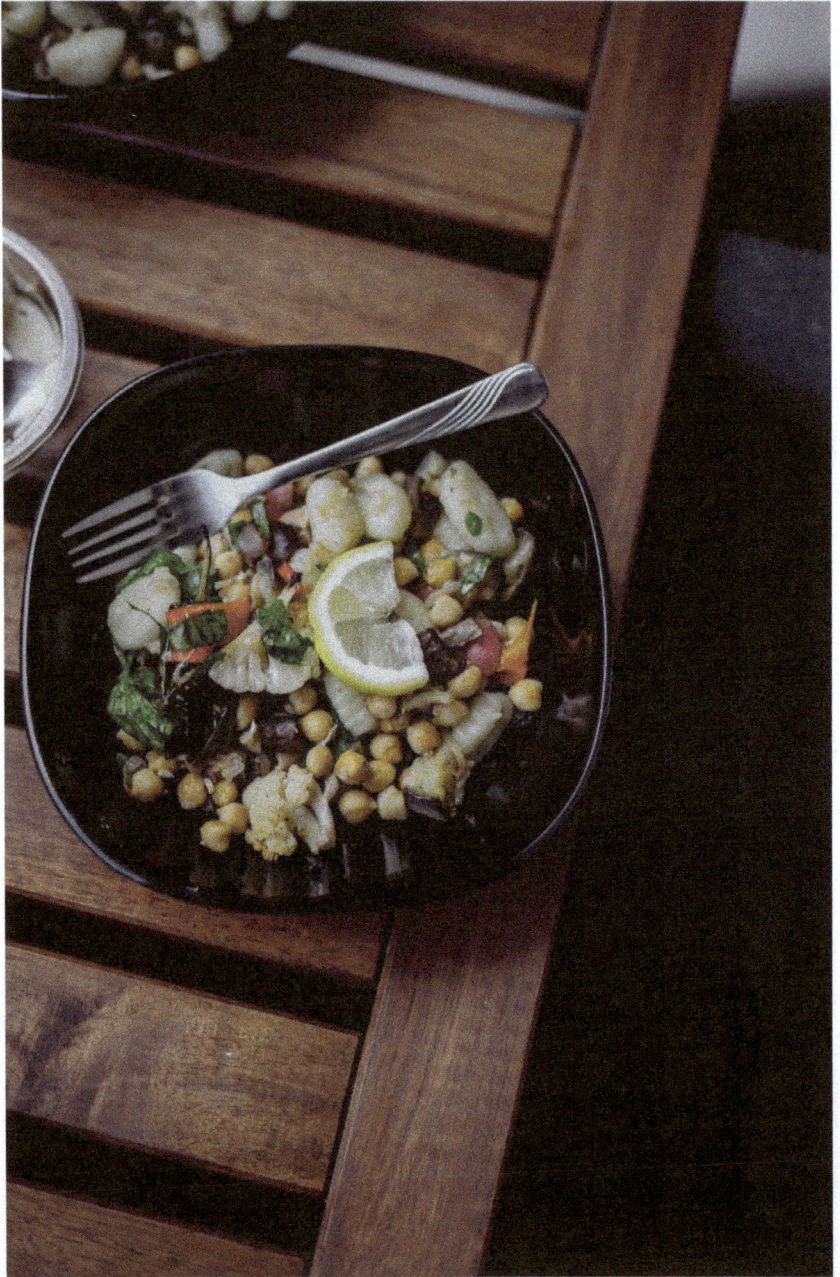

Conclusion

With the Ninja Foodie XL Grill Cookbook, you'll learn how to prepare the freshest food any way you like. You'll start with the basics and work your way up to more advanced techniques. With each technique, you'll get step-by-step instructions and helpful hints to make sure your foods turn out just right. Final Ninja Foodie XL Grill Tips:

- If you're new to grilling, start with the basics—the recipes are written for someone with minimal grilling experience.
- If you're a more advanced griller, feel free to use the recipes as a guide and make your own modifications.
- When you're grilling, always keep in mind that safety is the most important thing—if it seems like a recipe may be too complicated or you're not in a position to grill safely, then don't.
- Remember to grill in moderation and always have plenty of water on hand.
- Don't underestimate your Ninja Foodie XL Grill, especially when grilling.
- Have fun and enjoy the summer!

Tired of bland, boring grilled food? The Ninja Foodie XL Grill Cookbook is the perfect way to kickstart your grilling abilities. With great teaching tools like photos with every recipe and a large variety of recipes that range from basic to advanced and everything in between, you'll be well on your way to becoming a ninja griller.

If you own a Ninja Foodie XL Grill Cookbook, then you already know that it's more than just a grill cookbook. You've probably used it in ways that we never imagined. For instance, you may have used it to make "kabobs" by simply placing the meat on a skewer and cooking it on the grill. That's right! You just placed the meat on a skewer and cooked it!

But there's even more to the Ninja Foodie XL Grill Cookbook than this. You can use the cookbook to start your restaurant using your Ninja Foodie XL Grill Cookbook as a menu. You can even make food for customers right in your kitchen and then have them take it back to their homes with their own Ninja Foodie XL Grill Cookbook. This grill is for everyone no matter if he/she is a professional chef or a person who has just started to cook and wants to cook healthy food with no artificial preservatives added. Ninja Foodi Smart XL Grill is easy to use and will help you prepare your favorite recipes in minutes. It will inspire you to try new recipes as well. This grill comes with an excellent customer support service that will answer any question you might have within 24 hours. A smart grill that promises to cook food faster which is safer and healthier, enter the world of technology. From the name itself, Ninja Foodi Smart XL Grill is a grill that is smart and promises convenient for everyone to use. With this grill, it claims to cook meat in a healthy manner by emitting infrared heat from its dome-shaped lid. It sizzles the meat while leaving moisture and then results in a juicy flavor.

You can also use your Ninja Foodie XL Grill Cookbook to barbecue animals such as turkeys, chickens, and ducks on your grill. And you can roast marshmallows on your grill using your Ninja Foodie XL Grill Cookbook. You'll find all the Ninja Foodie XL Grill Cookbook tools that are necessary to do so inside of this cookbook! In conclusion, if you own a Ninja Foodie XL Grill Cookbook, then you'll see that it's more than just a grill cookbook; it's a tool that will allow you to experience many cooking techniques that we could never have imagined!

CPSIA information can be obtained
at www.ICGtesting.com
Printed in the USA
BVHW090027140521
607263BV00002B/60